GREAT PREDATORS

LION

by Marylou Morano Kjelle

Content Consultant
Bruce D. Leopold, PhD
Sharp Distinguished Professor of Wildlife Ecology
Mississippi State University

CORE
LIBRARY

Published by ABDO Publishing Company, PO Box 398166, Minneapolis, MN 55439. Copyright © 2014 by Abdo Consulting Group, Inc. International copyrights reserved in all countries. No part of this book may be reproduced in any form without written permission from the publisher. The Core Library™ is a trademark and logo of ABDO Publishing Company.

Printed in the United States of America,
North Mankato, Minnesota
052013
092013

♻ THIS BOOK CONTAINS AT LEAST 10% RECYCLED MATERIALS.

Editor: Lauren Coss
Series Designer: Becky Daum

Library of Congress Control Number: 2013932512

Cataloging-in-Publication Data
Kjelle, Marylou Morano.
 Lion / Marylou Morano Kjelle.
   p. cm. -- (Great Predators)
ISBN 978-1-61783-950-4 (lib. bdg.)
ISBN 978-1-62403-015-4 (pbk.)
Includes bibliographical references and index.
1. Lions--Juvenile literature. 2. Predatory animals--Juvenile literature.   I. Title.
599.757--dc23

                                        2013932512

Photo Credits: Thinkstock, cover, 1, 4, 7, 10, 12, 21, 34, 43; Nick Biemans/Shutterstock Images, 9; Jake Sorensen/Shutterstock Images, 14; Biosphoto/SuperStock, 16; NHPA/SuperStock, 18; FLPA/SuperStock, 22; Gerrit deVries/Shutterstock Images, 24; Peter Schwarz/Shutterstock Images, 26; Jos Beltman/Shutterstock Images, 28; Red Line Editorial, 30, 39; Leigh Murray/AP Images, 37; EastVillage Images/Shutterstock Images, 40, 45

CONTENTS

CHAPTER ONE

ON THE HUNT

Several adult zebras and their foals nibble peacefully on the grasses of the African savanna. They do not know that a pride, or family unit, of lions is close by. This is not a good time for the zebras to be grazing in the lions' territory. The lions are hungry. They are on the hunt for prey. One unlucky zebra is about to become dinner for the pride.

Lions often pick out weak and old animals that are easier to catch.

A lioness chooses a zebra. She picks a weak-looking zebra that is grazing apart from the rest. This zebra will be easier to overpower. The lioness crawls downwind from her prey. The zebra won't smell the lioness's scent and suspect danger. The lioness adds to the surprise attack by stretching herself flat on the ground. Her lightly spotted, tawny coat blends in well with the grass. She is almost completely camouflaged.

She slowly creeps on her belly toward her victim. If the lioness senses that the zebra knows she is near, she freezes. She waits quietly. Soon she can once again slide toward the zebra without being noticed.

Now other lionesses start taking up their positions. They slowly

Hungry Lions

The weight of the average kill is around 250 pounds (113 kg). A kill this size will feed six to eight lions. A full-grown lion can eat up to 75 pounds (34 kg) of food at a time. After eating this much food in one sitting, a lion that is not very active may not have to eat again for a few days. A lion can go four days without drinking water.

Lions are carnivores. They live on the flesh of other animals.

surround the zebra. Soon the zebra is trapped within
a circle of lions. Before long the first lioness is close
enough to strike. She leaps and pounces on the zebra
from behind. The other lionesses follow her lead.
Several jump on the zebra's back at the same time.
The zebra kicks and struggles to free itself. But the
lionesses' hook-like claws dig deep into its flesh. Soon
the lionesses overpower the zebra. They force it to

the ground. One lioness grasps the zebra's neck with her powerful jaws. The lionesses' pride will eat today.

Kings of the Savanna

Most lions stand between three and a half to four feet (1–1.2 m) tall. Adult males can weigh up to 550 pounds (250 kg). They may measure up to ten feet (3 m) long. Adult females weigh up to 400 pounds (180 kg). They measure up to nine feet (2.7 m) long. Most lions have gold or yellowish fur. This helps them blend in to the savanna's long grasses. Cubs often have spotted fur. Adult male lions have large manes around their heads.

Padded feet let a lion creep up quietly behind its prey and attack from behind. Large paws

Loud Lions

Lions make noise often. The loudest roars of male and female lions can be heard more than five miles (8 km) away. Male lions roar to show that they are in charge of a territory or to frighten competitors. Lions will also roar contentedly after eating a satisfying meal. Mother lions use grunts to communicate with their cubs.

Lionesses usually share their kill with the rest of the pride.

allow the lion to kill small prey with one crushing swipe. Powerful muscles and long legs give a lion the strength to move fast and pounce on its victim.

CHAPTER TWO

INSIDE THE PRIDE

Lions are tough hunters. But they are also social animals. Most lions live in groups called prides. A pride is made up of related lionesses, their cubs, and several dominant males. Some lion cubs will stay in the prides they were born in for life. A pride can be as big as 40 lions or as small as 3 lions.

When lionesses are about three years old, they are usually ready to mate. Males usually begin mating

A mother lion carries her young cubs in her mouth when she wants to move them from place to place.

Lion prides usually consist of a group of related females, such as mothers, sisters, and cousins, and a few unrelated males.

at about the age of five. They will mate with many different females over their lifetime. Lions do not have a mating season. They mate throughout the year. Most lionesses have a litter, or group, of cubs every two to three years. All the lionesses in a pride mate at the same time.

Females are pregnant with their cubs for about three and a half months. When it is time for the cubs to be born, the lioness leaves the pride. She moves to a safe place called a den. The den may be a cave or an area with heavy plant coverage. A lioness usually gives birth to a litter of up to four cubs. Each cub weighs approximately one pound (0.5 kg).

Life as a Cub

Lion cubs cannot see or walk for a few weeks after birth. Mother lions sometimes hide their cubs under rocks or in hollow trees or other protected areas. This keeps the cubs safe from hyenas, leopards, and other lions.

Males do not help raise cubs. But female members of a pride help each other raise their

Dangerous Dads

Some of the greatest dangers for lion cubs are adult male lions. When a new group of dominant males takes over a pride, one of the first things they do is kill all existing cubs. Males do not want to raise cubs that were fathered by other males. The male lions want the pride to be full of their own cubs. A lioness usually gives birth every two years. But she will do so sooner if her cubs die before the age of two. Lionesses try to protect their cubs from the male lions. But they are much smaller than the males, and they are rarely successful.

Lion cubs wrestle and play with one another in Botswana, Africa.

young. When one lioness needs to leave her young to hunt for meat, the other lionesses care for her cubs by feeding them and protecting them from predators. The cubs wrestle and play with the other cubs in their pride.

Lion cubs drink their mother's milk for the first three months. When they are six weeks old, the cubs begin eating small amounts of meat. Lion cubs are weaned when they are between six and eight months old. From this point on, the cubs only eat meat. Lion cubs learn to become predators by watching their mother and other adult lions hunt and kill. By the time they are two years old, young lions take an active part in hunting and killing prey.

Growing Up

Most lionesses will stay with their home prides for the rest of their lives. However, male lions are forced out of the pride when they are about three years old. All young males of the same age leave the pride together. They live in small groups, known as bachelor groups, until they are strong enough to take over an established pride. A group of lions take over a pride by challenging the pride's dominant male. The lions fight for control. Weaker lions usually don't survive

Lone Females

Most females remain in the pride for life. But some leave and become nomads. These lionesses travel from place to place and are usually not welcome to join other prides. Lionesses that leave the pride of their birth have to compete with other nomadic lions for food and shelter. Without the help of a pride, these lone lionesses usually do not survive long.

When they are old enough, male lions leave their pride in search of a new one.

the fight. If the new lions win, any surviving male lions must leave the pride. These lions will start looking for a new pride to take over.

A dominant male has two jobs. He must mate with all the females in the pride, and he must defend the pride from other males who want to take it over. Most males keep control of a pride for about four years. Because they are so often fighting for their lives, male lions don't live as long as females. On average, male lions live to be about 12 years old. Lionesses usually live for 15 to 18 years.

Ecologist Craig Packer has spent much of his life studying lions and their prides. In 2010 a writer from *Smithsonian Magazine* traveled to Tanzania to write about Packer's lion research there:

> *"What we wanted to do was figure out why they did some of these things," Packer says. "Why did they raise their cubs together? Did they really hunt cooperatively?"[Packer and his colleagues] kept tabs on two dozen prides in minute detail. . . . They noted where the lions congregated, who was eating how much of what, who had mated, who was wounded, who survived and who died. . . . They began to see how prides functioned. Members of a large pride didn't get any more to eat than a lone hunter. . . .Yet lions band together without fail to confront and sometimes kill intruders. Larger groups thus monopolize the premier savanna real estate.*

> *Source: Abigail Tucker. "The Truth about Lions." Smithsonian Magazine. Smithsonian Media, January 2010. Web. Accessed April 2, 2013.*

What's the Big Idea?

The author of the passage above is using evidence to support a point. Write a few sentences describing the point the author is making. Then write down two or three pieces of evidence the author uses to make the point.

CHAPTER THREE

BUILT TO KILL

Lions will eat almost any meat they can catch. They prefer large animals that can feed the entire pride, such as zebra, wildebeest, and antelope. They usually attack the smallest or weakest of these large animals for an easier kill. Lions also attack the young of even larger animals, such as elephants, giraffes, buffalos, rhinoceroses, and hippopotamuses. If they are starving, lions may go after adults of these

Lions are patient predators. They will watch their prey and wait for the right moment to strike.

animals. When large prey is hard to find, lions eat smaller animals, such as reptiles and rodents. If there is no live prey to be found, lions become scavengers. They eat carrion left behind by other predators, such as hyenas, cheetahs, or wild dogs. Sometimes lions steal fresh kills from these other predators.

Clever Hunters

Lions aren't always able to catch prey when they have to chase it for long distances. Lions can run about 30 miles (48 km) per hour for short periods of time. Many of the animals that lions prey on run faster. Lions make up for this disadvantage by waiting for the right time to attack their prey. This is called ambush hunting.

Lions know zebras and other animals need

Lazy Lions

Hunting, killing, and eating prey take hard work and energy. But lions spend most of their time resting. A lion is inactive almost 80 percent of the time. This adds up to about 20 hours a day. These hours are spent sleeping on rocks, alongside streams, or high in the branches of trees.

Lions try to surprise their prey, so they don't have to chase it for long distances.

water to survive. Lions often stake out watering holes and ambush thirsty animals. Lions also chase herds of wildebeests or zebras when they are crossing rivers. These animals cannot run as fast in water as they can on land. The lion has an easier kill. Some young prey, such as warthog piglets, burrow into the soft earth

Lions have excellent night vision, so they are often active after dark.

for protection. Lions dig until they find the piglet and then kill and eat it.

Lions prefer to hunt at night, especially when there is no moon. Lions have good night vision, which allows them to see well in dark conditions. The prey is less likely to see the lions. There is more opportunity for a surprise attack.

Lions are well equipped for life as predators. They have a strong sense of smell and a sharp sense of hearing, both of which help locate prey. A lion can hear prey from one mile (1.6 km) away. Like other cats, lions have retractable claws. These claws act like hooks. Lions use their claws for capturing and holding on to prey. Lions also use their claws for climbing trees and for fighting other animals. A lion keeps its claws sharp by rubbing and scraping them against a tree trunk. The claws also stay sharp because they remain in the lion's footpad when not needed.

Male Hunters

For many years, researchers believed most male lions relied on lionesses for their food. However, a recent study suggests that some male lions are also powerful hunters. Researchers observed male lions hunting at night in areas with dense vegetation. Researchers had not explored these areas in the past because the thick plant cover made them difficult to study. Females were more likely to hunt in groups in open areas. The male lions were more likely to hunt alone and ambush their prey.

Lions have sharp teeth they use to kill and eat their prey.

Lions have four dagger-like canine teeth. Two are on the top of the lion's mouth, and two are on the bottom. Lions use these teeth to kill their prey. Canine teeth are also used to bite an opponent when lions fight one another.

A Team Effort

Lionesses work together as a team to supply food for the pride. The pride's oldest lioness takes the lead. The lionesses cooperate to corner and kill their prey.

Once the animal is dead, the lionesses gather around the body. They tear at the flesh with special teeth called carnassial molars. These teeth cut through skin, tendons, and bones to get to the meat. The teeth cut the meat into smaller pieces. Then the lions swallow these chunks of meat whole. The lion's tongue is rough, like sandpaper. It scrapes the prey's meat from the bone.

The lionesses work together to hunt and kill prey. But they do not like to share their meal. Fierce fights sometimes break out as they compete for the meat.

Male lions usually eat before the other members of a pride.

A male lion often wrestles the carcass away from the lionesses. He drags it to another area to eat most of the carcass himself. After the male has had his fill, he then allows the females to eat what is left.

Lion cubs must also fight for their share of the meat. They eagerly gobble up any scraps that the adults don't finish. But adult lions make sure their own

FURTHER EVIDENCE

Chapter Three covers how lions hunt and their predatory characteristics. If you could pick out the main point of Chapter Three, what would it be? What are some pieces of evidence used to support this point? The Web site at the link below also discusses lions' hunting strategies. Find a quote from the Web site that supports Chapter Three's main point. Does the quote support an existing piece of evidence? Or does it provide new evidence?

How Lions Hunt

www.mycorelibrary.com/lion

cubs get enough to eat. Sometimes multiple animals are caught at the same time. Then there is plenty of food for all.

CHAPTER FOUR

THE LION'S HABITAT

At one time lions lived throughout most of Africa, large parts of Europe, and Asia. Now they live mainly in sub-Saharan and eastern Africa. A small population of lions lives in a small, forested area of India. African lions live in grasslands, savannas, dense bush, and open woodlands. They don't live in deserts or humid rainforests.

Most lions live in African grasslands and open woodlands.

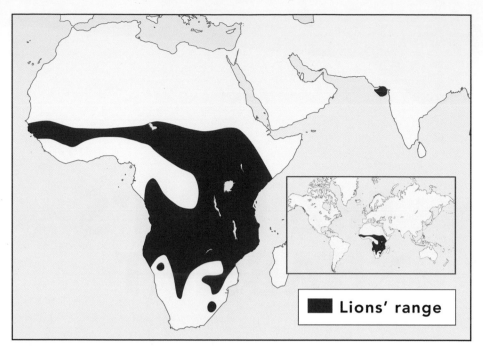

Lions' Range Map

Today wild lions live in Africa and India. The map above shows the regions that lions call home. After reading about the lions' habitat, why do you think lions thrive in these parts of the world?

The geographical region where an animal population lives is called its range. Lions' African range areas experience rainy and dry seasons. These seasons vary in different parts of Africa.

In the woodlands, the rainy season forces the lions' prey to leave the range in search of food. The lions must look farther and wider to satisfy their hunger. With fewer prey to hunt and kill, lions may go for longer periods without food. In the dry season, many of the lions' prey animals return to the lions' range. The lions have plenty of food to eat.

Lions' Territories

The area within a range where a pride lives is its territory. The size of the pride determines the size of the territory. A territory needs to have enough zebra, antelope, and other prey to support all the lions in the pride. There also has to be a watering hole, river, or stream to provide drinking water. Lastly, a territory needs to have shelter. Trees, caves, and rock piles protect lions from hot sun, drenching rains, and territory intruders.

Ancient Lions

As long as 13,000 years ago, ancient relatives of modern lions lived all over the world. Researchers have found evidence of these ancient lions in North America, the United Kingdom, and mainland Europe. The scientists believe these lions may have been 25 percent larger than African lions. The ancient lions likely lived alongside wooly mammoths and saber-tooth tigers.

Where Did the European Lions Go?

At one time, lions lived in many parts of Europe. Scientists aren't certain what happened to European lions. But many believe a changing landscape and climate may have been partially to blame. Thousands of years ago, forests spread throughout Europe. This made it difficult for lions to continue living in these areas. Many of the large animals the lions preyed on could not survive in the forest. European lions had to follow their prey to other areas with more favorable living conditions to survive. As the human population expanded in Europe, lions may also have been overhunted.

When food is plentiful, this territory averages about 15 square miles (39 sq km) in size. When food is scarce, a pride might expand its territory to 100 square miles (260 sq km). The pride needs more space to hunt and kill enough food for all pride members.

A dominant male lion marks the boundaries of his territory by urinating on them. He also roars to scare away competing lions and other animals. Lions belonging to a pride sometimes break into

EXPLORE ONLINE

The focus of Chapter Four is lions' range and habitat. The video at the Web site below also discusses lions' habitat and why they might be well suited to it. As you know, every source is different. How is the information given on the Web site different from the information in this chapter? What information is the same? How do the two sources present this information differently?

Lion Habitats
www.mycorelibrary.com/lion

smaller groups. These groups travel to different parts of the territory. But most often members of a pride stay together in one general area.

CHAPTER FIVE

FIGHTING FOR SURVIVAL

Lions have few natural predators in the wild. Old lions that are no longer part of a pride and too weak to hunt or scavenge may starve to death. Many lions die from injuries they receive from attacking prey or fighting other lions. Weak and sick lions are preyed on by hyenas and wild dogs. Other large predators, such as leopards, prey on lion cubs. But by far, the lion's most dangerous threat is humans.

Healthy adult lions have no natural predators besides other lions.

Masai Hunters

The Masai are a group of nomadic people who live in east Africa. Lion hunting has been an important part of Masai culture for thousands of years. Masai hunters use spears to kill lions. And they are not allowed to hunt lionesses, cubs, or male lions that are starving or weak.

Lion Hunting

Lions are protected from hunting in many parts of Africa. But it is legal to hunt lions in many other parts of Africa. Lion hunters need a special license. Most countries require the hunter to travel with a local guide. In many places, it is illegal to hunt females and cubs. And only a certain number of males can be killed each year. These laws help make sure that hunting does not threaten the wild lion population.

However, some hunters, known as poachers, hunt lions illegally. Lion teeth and other parts of a lion's body sell for a lot of money. Lion bones are popular in certain medicines produced in Asia. Poachers sneak these bones out of Africa to sell illegally. Sometimes

For Masai boys and men, killing a lion is seen as an important part of becoming an adult.

lions get caught in wire traps poachers set for other animals. The trapped lions often starve to death.

Habitat Loss

Today people live in areas where few humans lived in the past. Human-made structures now exist where open land used to be. People have built roads, buildings, and cities on what was once the lions' habitat. Neither lions nor their prey can survive on the developed land. And people generally do not want to live or work in areas where lions or other large predators roam.

The increase of farms and ranches in former wilderness areas has also impacted the lion population. Given the

Asiatic Lions

One of the most threatened lion populations is the group of lions living in western India. These Asiatic lions are shaggier than African lions, and they have larger tassels on their tails. At one time, the lions roamed many parts of Europe and Asia. Today most live in the Gir Forest National Park and Wildlife Sanctuary in Gujarat, India. Scientists believe there are approximately 400 Asiatic lions left in the wild.

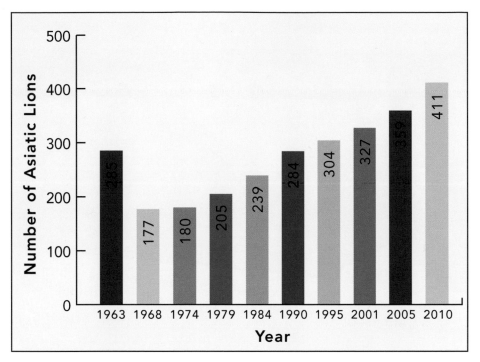

Asiatic Lion Population in India's Gir Forest

Asiatic lions are extremely threatened. However, the population of the Asiatic Lion in the Gir Forest began rising in the mid-1970s. It has been on the increase ever since. What are some of the factors that you learned about in this book that might have contributed to this increase? What can humans do to help the lion population continue to grow?

opportunity and need, a lion will prey on cattle and other livestock. Many farmers intentionally poison lions to protect their animals.

Because of these threats, the lions' population has been reduced dramatically in the last 100 years. Scientists estimate there are approximately 32,000

Today most lions live on wildlife preserves where hunting is banned or restricted, such as Serengeti National Park.

lions left in the wild. Many scientists worry that hunting and habitat loss will continue hurting the lions' populations.

Many people now realize the value of lions and other predators. Today most of the world's lions live in park reserves. These are special sections of land where lions are protected from hunting and human development. The safety and protection of habitats like these will help the lion remain the top predator of the savanna for many years to come.

In 2013 Alexander N. Songorwa, Tanzania's director of wildlife, wrote an editorial in response to the US Fish and Wildlife Service's announcement that it was considering placing lions on the endangered species list:

> *Odd as it may sound, American trophy hunters play a critical role in protecting wildlife in Tanzania. The millions of dollars that hunters spend to go on safari here each year help finance the game reserves, wildlife management areas and conservation efforts in our rapidly growing country.*
>
> *This is why we are alarmed that the United States Fish and Wildlife Service is considering listing the African lion as endangered. Doing so would make it illegal for American hunters to bring their trophies home. Those hunters constitute 60 percent of our trophy-hunting market, and losing them would be disastrous to our conservation efforts.*

Source: Alexander N. Songorwa. "Saving Lions by Killing Them." New York Times. New York Times Company, March 17, 2013. Web. Accessed April 2, 2013.

Changing Minds

Take a position on lion hunting in Tanzania. Imagine that your best friend has the opposite opinion. Write an editorial trying to change your friend's mind. Make sure you explain your opinion and your reasons for it. Include facts and details that support your reasons.

FAST FACTS

Common Name: Lion

Scientific Name: *Panthera leo*

Average Size: Males are usually nine feet (2.7 m) long; females are usually eight feet (2.4 m) long

Average Weight: Males are typically 350 to 400 pounds (157–180 kg); females weigh 250 pounds (113 kg)

Color: Yellow or gold

Average Lifespan: 12 years for males; 15 to 18 years for females

Diet: Usually large prey, such as zebra, wildebeest, and antelope; occasionally eat smaller animals and carrion left behind by other predators

Habitat: Lions live only in Africa and India in grasslands, savannas, dense bush, and open woodlands

Predators: Other lions and humans; hyenas, leopards, and other large predators prey on cubs

Did You Know?

- A lion's roar can be heard for a distance of five miles (8 km).
- The largest lion was recorded to be nearly 700 pounds (318 kg) and nearly 11 feet (3 m) long.
- Lions can run 30 miles (48 km) an hour.

Tell the Tale

Chapter Two talks about lion cubs growing up. Write 200 words that tell the story of a group of young male lions leaving the pride for the first time. Where do they go? What do they do? Make sure to set the scene, develop a sequence of events, and include a conclusion.

Dig Deeper

After reading this book, what questions do you still have about lions? Maybe you want to know more about pride life or lions' hunting habits. Write down a few questions that can guide you in doing research. Ask an adult to help you find a reliable source to help you answer your questions. Then write a paragraph about how you did your research and what you learned from it.

Say What?

Learning about predators can mean learning a lot of new vocabulary. Find five words in this book that you have never seen or heard before. Use a dictionary to find out what they mean. Then write the meanings in your own words, and use each word in a sentence.

Why Do I Care?

Chapter Five of this book talks about how the population of lions has declined in the last 100 years. Even if you don't live near the lions' habitat, why should you care about their decline? Write a short essay discussing why lions are important predators.

GLOSSARY

camouflage
patterns or coloring that help disguise or hide an animal

carcass
an animal's dead body

carrion
dead and rotting flesh

mane
long, thick hair that grows around a male lion's neck

nomad
a person or animal that wanders without settling down in one place

poacher
someone who collects or hunts an animal illegally

retractable
able to be pulled inside of something else

savanna
tropical or subtropical grassland area with scattered trees and shrubs

scavenger
an animal that eats animals that are already dead

tawny
yellowish in color

wean
stop drinking mother's milk

LEARN MORE

Books

Hoare, Ben, and Tom Jackson. *Endangered Animals.* New York: DK Publishing, 2010.

Joubert, Beverly, and Dereck Joubert. *Face to Face with Lions.* Washington, DC: National Geographic, 2008.

Shah, Anup. *Serengeti Spy: Views from a Hidden Camera on the Plains of East Africa.* New York: Abrams, 2012.

Web Links

To learn more about lions, visit ABDO Publishing Company online at **www.abdopublishing.com**. Web sites about lions are featured on our Book Links page. These links are routinely monitored and updated to provide the most current information available.
Visit **www.mycorelibrary.com** for free additional tools for teachers and students.

INDEX

ABOUT THE AUTHOR

Marylou Morano Kjelle is a college English professor, freelance writer, and photojournalist who lives and works in Central New Jersey.